The Hauntings of Mitchell

Ryan Murtoff

Table of Contents

Foreword

As far back as I can remember, I have always had things happen around me that I cannot explain. I said it was ghosts, but it was often dismissed as the overactive imagination of a young child or me just wanting extra attention. Others made fun of me while I was little and people to this day still try to explain away these events of my life. Some question whether I use illegal drugs or if I have been tested for sleep paralysis. To all the nay-sayers, it is easy for you to pass judgement when you have never experienced anything paranormal. My hope is that by writing everything down and telling my story, people will understand what I have gone through for most of my life. Maybe someone will be able to shed some light on my experiences and explain the why and what of these events that have and continue to happen to me up to this day. I have talked with a few people about these events in my life. They believe me and give me advice. They believe I am gifted and a "sensitive" at the very least. A sensitive is a person that is very in tune with the spiritual realm and can notice entities in any environment. They recommend that I talk with a professional at some point for better spiritual guidance. I hope you enjoy reading my stories of the true paranormal events of my life.

Mitchell Ryan Murtoff

2023

The Beginning

My paranormal experiences began at a very early age. I believe I was around five years old or so. I would walk through my parents' house, and I would hear my name called in a voice that I did not recognize. I would check with my mom, dad, or brother to see if they called me. Everyone would say no. They would say I must be hearing things. This continued for some time at my parents' house. Every time, they would say it was not them. Occasionally they would tell me to stop pretending or playing games with them. Things began to settle down for a little bit as I stopped paying attention to the voice. The house was built brand new in 1962 and my parents were the first people to live in it.

A couple of years went by without any major happenings. When I was about seven or so, my parents let my brother move into another room; we had shared a bedroom up to this point. My room is located on the back side of the house with a covered porch on the outside with a double window.

During the summertime when I was not in school or playing baseball, I would play with my G.I. Joe toys or Transformers on the floor. My mom would have the windows open to help keep the house cool since we did not have air conditioning. The drapes would also be pulled back to let the sun light in the house. My room did not get a lot of sunlight, but there was enough coming in the window to help light up my room. There would be a cool breeze that came through my room during the day. We lived in a quiet neighborhood. During the summer, most of the noise came from the neighbors mowing their grass or the occasional train passing by. There are a set of railroad tracks that run at the back edge of the property line.

This is when things started happening again. Almost every day I would be playing with my G.I. Joes or Transformers on the floor, when out of nowhere, I would see shadows of three people being cast on the inside wall of my bedroom coming from the back porch. I would not hear any footsteps. I would just get a feeling and look up and see the shadows. I would get up and look out my window. No one was around. I went outside and looked around the sides of the house, sometimes walking the whole way around the house and I could not find anyone. This would happen every day, sometimes several times a day. I did not know what to do other than to keep watch and try to catch the people walking around the house.

One day, I was in my room and got that feeling again and looked at my wall. It was the shadows on my wall. This time they stopped and looked at me, then continued moving. I ran outside to see them but there was no one there. I sprinted around the house and could not find anyone. I ran to the backyard and looked toward the factory that was on the other side of the railroad tracks. No one was there. It was like they were letting me know I was being watched and there was nothing I could do about it.

Another scary incident occurred one evening at my parents' house. I had finished eating dinner and was on my way to my room; my parents and brother were still eating dinner. For some reason, I felt drawn to the basement. I opened the door to the basement and closed the door. Then, I laid down on the top step and proceeded to log roll down the entire flight of steps (11 steps) and landed on the basement floor. I hit my head on the concrete floor and was slightly dazed. My parents came running down the steps and wanted to know what happened and why I did that. I could not answer at first and then said, "I don't know why I did that." They made sure I was OK and helped me to my feet. They kept an eye on me for the rest of the evening and night. This was an isolated incident when I was young.

The basement stairwell that I log rolled down.

Once, it was coming up on Labor Day weekend. My brother and I always helped my mom and dad get ready for vacation. Every Labor Day and Memorial Day weekend, we would go camping at Mill Bridge Village campground in Lancaster, Pennsylvania. We would meet my Uncle Laird and Aunt Linda there along with my cousins, Kim, and Penny. We would always camp in sites that were side by side. My parents and aunt and uncle would reserve the same sites almost every year that went. We would ride bikes or go for walks through the campground all the time.

This particular incident occurred on a camp site that bordered the corn field of an Amish farm. One day after riding my bike for a couple of hours, I was very tired and wanted to take a nap. I told my parents that I was going to lie down and rest for a while. They said OK and remained outside the camper with everyone else. I climbed up into the bunk of the camper and laid down. It was not long until I fell asleep. I was out cold for some time, then it happened. I heard someone say, "Mitchell, Mitchell." It was a man's voice that I did not recognize. This happened a couple of times before I did anything. I sat straight up and hit my head on the ceiling of the camper. Then, I looked out the window and asked my mom and dad if anyone had called for me. They said no. I thought I might have been dreaming at first. I laid back down and started to doze off, now with a headache from hitting my head on the ceiling.

After a couple of minutes, it happened again. I heard, "Mitchell, Mitchell" in the same man's voice. Once again, I leaned towards the window and asked everyone out there if anyone had said my name or wanted me to come outside. It was the same result. No one had called me for anything. I laid back down again and was getting worried. I had just laid back down when I heard it again, "Mitchell, Mitchell." There was more urgency in the voice this time. It was louder and more intense. This time I was wide awake. I looked around and did not see anyone in the camper and looked out the window quickly. Everyone had left the campsites. I really was not sure what to do. I was raised in a fundamentalist Baptist church, Faith Chapel of Carlisle, PA. We had been studying the Old Testament and how sometimes God would talk directly with people.

I thought I would give this a try. I said, "Yes Lord, I am listening." That was the last time I heard that voice.

Once we returned home from this camping trip, the activity continued and picked up in intensity. I would be in the living room watching TV or reading a book and the door at the end of the hallway would open. (I always read lots of books when I was younger.) This was the door to my brother's room. I thought he was in his room and was coming out into the living room. No one would come through the door. After several times, I walked through the house and looked in the room. There was no one there. I would say "Hello," and there was no response. The room is completely enclosed. There is only one door going in or out of the room. There are also two windows. I thought maybe he was messing with me at first. One evening, I got that feeling again like I was not alone. I looked at the door and saw the doorknob turn and the door swung wide open. This time it opened almost the whole way. I looked and saw an empty room. The more I thought about it, the more I started to believe in the paranormal. The door opening by itself continued daily for several years, in some cases, several times a day. I would always look to make sure no one was there.

The door at the end of the hall always opened by itself. The handle would turn, and the door would swing wide open.

Things were continuing to happen around the house. The shadows would still appear on a regular basis as well as the door opening by itself. Something changed when I was 13 years old. One Sunday morning, I was getting ready to go to church. I got in the shower like normal. I had a hard time holding the soap. It was like I had almost no power in my hands. They started trembling and the soap would fall out of my hands. This happened several times and made lots of noise since we used bars of soap growing up. (Safeguard, I believe.). My brother was in the hallway and came in to check on me. I said I was OK and was just having a hard time holding onto the soap. Then things got worse as I was getting ready to wash my hair. My arms began to move uncontrollably at my shoulders. The bottle of shampoo would go flying out of my hands. After that happened, everything went black. When I came to, I was in the back of the ambulance. I was completely out of it. Once I arrived at the hospital, they began running all kinds of tests on me including an EEG and an EKG. They determined that I had a grand maul seizure. I was immediately put on Depakote to control the epilepsy. After this, the activity stopped for many years. It is like the medication somehow changed something.

It took several days for me to recover from the seizure. I was no longer seeing the shadows and the door had stopped opening. I was different. The seizure had some type of impact on my brain. I did not get the uneasy feelings I used to get before the activity occurred. In fact, nothing happened for a long time.

Then, the door started opening again. This started to reoccur when I was about 16 or so. I would never see anything or anyone around the door when it happened. Now, I would just react to hearing the doorknob turn. I would still look and find no one in the room. Most of the time, this would happen when I was by myself. I would still go into the room and investigate to see if someone had broken into the house or if someone was hiding in the closet. I started to get an uneasy feeling in the room when I investigated. It was hard to explain. It felt like someone was there with me or I was being watched. They did not want me in the room, but my curiosity always got the better of me.

This game of cat and mouse continued until I was 18 or 19 years old. My neurologist thought I might outgrow my seizures, so he recommended that I stop taking my medication. I took four pills a day at the time, (and still do). I would gradually go off the medication. The plan was to cut back by one pill a day per month until I was not taking any at all. Everything was going well until I was almost off the prescription. I was getting ready for church one Sunday morning and went to get into the shower like normal. I started to have trouble holding the soap again. It would go flying out of my hands. My shoulders were twitching uncontrollably, making my arms jump. This time, my family got me out of the shower and onto my bed. They rolled me over onto my stomach. I laid for several minutes until the seizure stopped. Later that day, they contacted my neurologist and informed him of what had happened. He immediately put me back on my medication again. I went through the same adjustment period as the last time. After several days, I was feeling "normal" again. The paranormal activity stopped again.

In the fall of 1993, I left for college. I lived on campus at Elizabethtown College in Ober Hall on Ober A-1. I made a lot of great friends there. I began to party almost every weekend. I had a roommate. We had gone to high school together and graduated together. The overall feeling of the campus was completely different than at my parents' house. While I was on campus, I did not get any feelings of uneasiness or unrest like I did when I was at my parents' house. As a result, I would rarely go home on the weekends. I was enjoying spending time with my new friends. This new sense of freedom lifted my spirits. I was at peace while I was there and did not have any paranormal experiences. I attended this college from the fall of 1993 until the spring of 1994. I had to take a year off due to academic reasons and then went back for another semester in the spring of 1995. After that semester, I moved back to my parents' house.

A noteworthy event happened during the summer of 1994. I played on the men's volleyball team while I attended Elizabethtown College. I became great friends with most of the guys on the team. I spent a lot of time training with one of my teammates. His name was

Brian. He was from southern New Jersey. He invited me to his house for a weekend. He said we could play beach volleyball at the local beach. I was super excited. We agreed on a weekend for me to visit. I drove there on a Friday evening. The next day we headed to the beach which was about 10 minutes from his parents' house. We played all day in a round robin tournament. I had excelled at indoor volleyball but struggled in the deep sand for the first few matches. I became sunburnt. I was not used to the intensity of the sun of the ocean.

On Sunday morning, I went to mass with Brian even though I am not Catholic. It was at the end of the service when we went to leave, we stopped to put some Holy Water on us. My face was bright red with sunburn. I used my finger to put some on my forehead. I looked in the mirror in the restroom and saw a dark red imprint of my finger on my forehead; it stood out from the sunburn. I thought this was unusual but eventually forgot about it. I mentioned it later to a couple of my friends that I discussed the paranormal events in my life with, and they told me that was a sign that I had been possessed at least twice.

I commuted to Messiah College from the fall of 1996 to the spring of 2000. During my time at this college, I also worked part-time at O'Malley Wood Products, often put in 16-hour days between classes, work, and homework. There were many sleepless nights. The door would continue to open on a regular basis during this time. The main difference between this time and when I was younger was that it always happened late at night. I would be in my bedroom working on homework and projects and I would be absorbed in my assignments and would hear the doorknob turn loudly. I would go check to see if it was my mom or dad going into the room or if there was an intruder. Every time I looked, no one was around. My mom and dad were sound asleep in their bed. My brother had moved out of the house several years ago, so was just me and my parents. I would look around in the room and then close the door. I would go to bed around midnight or 1 A.M. and sleep till about 6 A.M. or so before I had to get up and get ready to go to school. The interesting thing was nothing ever happened when I was on campus. The activity always happened at my parents' house. I was trying to figure things as to why this always happened when I was at the house. I wondered if it was residual or if someone was watching over me. For a while, I thought it was residual because it was always the same door, simply different times of the day.

I had a cat, named Charcoal for several years during this time. He was dropped off at the house several years ago on New Year's Eve. He was solid black. He was barely 8 weeks old when I found him in front of the house when my parents and I arrived back home from visiting my Uncle Dave and Aunt Bev's house. He never reacted to anything happening in the house. Then again, he was both an indoor and outdoor cat. He was not always in the house. He would go outside every night before we went to bed.

I had Charcoal for several years. Unfortunately, one night when he was crossing the road, he was hit and killed by a tractor trailer. I was heartbroken. There was an uptake in activity in the house when this happened. I do not think it was a coincidence. My sorrow fed the activity. The door would open several times a night. Each time I would look and then close the door when I did not see anyone in the room.

A few months later, I was with my mom and dad in the North Hanover Mall. I was walking by myself while they were shopping. I found myself wandering down a branch of the mall and ended up in a pet store. I walked around pondering whether to get another pet. They had fish, snakes, dogs, and other animals. I already had some fish from my time at Elizabethtown College. I had two Oscars, a red belly piranha, and a large algae eater. I really could not provide enough time and attention for a dog. I also did not want to go through the potty-training process and I knew my parents did not want another dog.

I was getting ready to leave when I saw the large cage with cats. One cat caught my eye. He was solid black. I picked him up and held him like a baby. I wanted to take him home so bad. I did not have the money to buy him on my own. I put him back in the cage and left the store to meet up with mom and dad. I found them waiting for me on a bench in the middle of the mall. They asked if I was ready to go and I told them I wanted to show them something. They followed me to the pet store, and I showed them the cat. I pleaded with them to help me buy him. After talking it over, they agreed to pay half. He would be my birthday present for that year. We took him home and I named him Cinder.

Once he got a little older, I could tell he was different from my other cat Charcoal. He would notice things happening in the house more. This could just be my perception because he was in the house all the time. He would always look towards the door at the end of the hallway. When it opened, he would crouch down to the floor and sneak towards the doorway. He would slowly enter the room and smell the floor. Then, he would run out of the room and come right to me and get close to me. It was like he was afraid of something. This became his routine whenever the door opened.

Cinder was always by my side when I was home. He would sleep with me every night. There were nights I would feel him moving around on my bed. At first, I did not think too much of it. I thought he was just trying to get settled or getting down to use the litter box. Then, one night I started to get an uneasy, restless feeling and felt him moving on my bed again. This time, I rolled over onto my side facing the wall with my dresser and hamper. I looked and saw him staring at the wall behind the hamper. I touched him and he did not move. He was fixated on something. I stared and investigated the darkness, and I could not see anything. He would stay there at attention like he was guarding me. After several minutes, the uneasy feeling subsided. I put my arm around him to hold him against me and then he moved. He snuggled against me. This would happen more frequently in the coming months.

I began to hear noises in my room not long after this started happening. It would sound like something was moving across my floor or on my bookshelf. I would look and everything was in place. I would look to see if Cinder had gotten off my bed or was walking around in my room. He would be lying beside me sound asleep. This started to bother me since I could not see anything in my room. This always happened at night when I tried to sleep.

There was also activity during the day when I would be at home. I was hardly ever home during the weekdays, and I would spend most weekends on campus working on homework or group projects for some of my classes. On the days I was home, I would be in my room working on schoolwork when out of nowhere, I would hear very loud scratching sounds on the wall in my bedroom where the hamper and dresser were. It would start at the top of the wall and go the whole way to the bottom. I would pull my dresser and hamper away from the wall and look for anything that could explain the noise. Every time I looked, there would be nothing there.

I would also check the wall for marks or scratches, but I never would find anything to explain it. This started to concern me. I had heard demons would often mark people with scratches. If one were marking that wall, I knew I would have a fundamental problem on my hand. I never discussed these events with anyone at college since it was a Christian college. Some people were already wary of spending time with me once they found out that I had attended Elizabethtown College. They were and still are bitter rivals. I was told not to tell anyone that I had attended Elizabethtown College.

In the spring of 2000, I began my internship with the Harrisburg Horizon, a semi-pro basketball team. I worked in their front office located near Lancaster, PA. The team was owned by an older couple. The team played its games at the Penn State Harrisburg campus. Players on the team were from Pennsylvania and other surrounding states like New Jersey and New York. I would work during the week at their office and do game day setup on the weekends. It was a wonderful experience. I met players from several states and enjoyed working with them. One of the players, Speedy Williams, had even starred in the movie Above the Rim. He gave me an autographed jersey and ball from one of the other teams he played on, The Harlem Wizards.

To fulfill my college requirements, I opted to study abroad for one semester. I decided to study in England. Normally this was done in the J-term or January term of the spring semester; however, this year it was moved to May and June due to concerns with Y2K. I was excited to go. I had never flown before so this would be a first for me.

We left in mid-May and flew into Heathrow airport. We spent the next month or so touring the country. We would visit churches, Cathedrals, museums, and other historical sites such as Stonehenge and Avebury. We did have some free travel time, during which I went to Scotland for five days. It was great to see all the architecture of the castles and historical buildings. I thought for sure that something would happen during this trip. To my surprise, nothing happened. I was disappointed but also relieved. I did not want to have to explain any paranormal experiences to this group of people.

We arrived back in the US about mid-June. I lived another week or so at my parents' house before moving to Columbus, Ohio to begin life on my own. Out of the four years I attended Messiah College, nothing paranormal ever happened to me while I was on campus. It always occurred at my parents' house.

The Ohio Years

In April of 2000, I went out to visit my friends Don and James and James' wife Maribeth (Mitzi) in Columbus, Ohio. I fell in love with the city right away. There was so much to do and so many people from different countries. It was a melting pot of diversity. I decided that I wanted to move out there once I completed college. Don helped me get a job interview with the company he worked at. The manager offered me the job on the spot. I explained to him that I would not be moving to Columbus until mid-June. He told me that he would hold the job for me until then. Don was living in a studio apartment at *The Club at Eagle's Point* in Reynoldsburg, a suburb of Columbus. We decided to rent a two-bedroom apartment in the same complex when I moved out there.

A week after returning to the US from England, my parents helped me to move to Columbus about mid to late June. Don's parents and brother also helped with the move. We moved into the two-bedroom apartment on the other side of the apartment complex from his studio apartment. Things were going great. Don and I were working a lot of hours and had the same schedule. We would often spend our days golfing on the golf course at the apartment complex or spending time with James and Maribeth. There was no paranormal activity in the apartment up to this point.

A few months later, Don married a girl from the Philippines. He flew over there to get her, and she moved into the apartment. At first, everything was great, then the energy shifted in the apartment. I began to feel uneasy whenever I was alone in the apartment with Don's wife. I did not say anything to Don. He was not aware of the encounters I had in my parents' house growing up. Something seemed off but I could not put my finger on it. A couple of months later, they got a dog. It was a black cocker spaniel they named Lady. That helped with the energy in the apartment for a while.

We lived in the apartment for about a year. Then we moved into a townhome in McNaughton Woods on the other side of Reynoldsburg. It was a significant improvement for us. It was a two-story townhome with a finished basement in a gated community. The extra space helped to alleviate some of the negative energy that was building up at the old apartment. Each bedroom had a master bathroom which was nice.

A few months into the lease, there was a major shift in the energy in the apartment. Things were becoming extremely negative. This energy was being focused on me. Don's wife had become very jealous of our friendship. Occasionally, there would be noises coming from the basement during the middle of the night. I would open the door to my bedroom and go downstairs to make sure everything was OK. I would go down there, and the lights would be off with nobody around. I began to think something from my parents' house had followed me out there.

Not long after this started, Don's wife became extremely angry with me when the maid of honor from their wedding came to visit from New York. I was holding hands with her and that was all that happened. She had washed some of her clothes while she was visiting and had asked me if she could hang them in my bathroom to dry. I said, "No problem." Don's wife came into my room the next day to ask me something and saw her friend's clothes hanging in my bathroom. This sent her over the edge. She did not ask for an explanation. She went on a yelling tirade so bad that I went down to the basement and could still hear her yelling like she was right next to me. The anger and pure hatred were palpable. The noises were also picking up in frequency and intensity. The energy was feeding off her negativity. A few weeks later I moved in with a coworker at my new job. It was a big relief to not have to deal with her anymore.

I moved into the townhome with Chris, my coworker, and his roommate Sean close to the fall of 2001, I think. We lived close to Bexley, a well-to-do suburb of Columbus. The complex we lived in was not in a good section of town though. We kept to ourselves. The atmosphere was light in the townhome. We watched a lot of Comedy Central and played X-Box. We also drank heavily. It was an adjustment for me going to a positive environment. Our friend and coworker, Ryan, would come to visit frequently. Chris, Ryan, and I always had a blast. My personality had started to change. I became more outgoing and crazier or wild. This would help me out immensely since I was an introvert most of my life. Chris and I also played softball together as on several teams while we lived together.

After living there for a year, something really changed with me, besides my personality. I began to pick up things going on in the townhome. It was like I became more open. I would sometimes hear voices when there was no one around. I would look out my window to see if anyone was in the parking lot walking around and there would be no one there. There were times when I felt like I lost control of myself and had left the townhome. A tidal wave of energy would engulf me, and I would stand facing one wall in my bedroom and bend both my arms at the elbow and then would turn my palms towards the ceiling. I could feel my eyes roll back in my head and my eyelids would close and I would speak. "There were 8 of us." Sometimes I would even repeat myself. I do not know where this came from.

I had no context for the phrase. Once I was done speaking, it was like I came back from somewhere and had to look around to see where I was. It was like lost time, but I did not remember saying it at first. A few hours later it would pop into my head, mostly just after I had laid down to go to sleep. This would happen almost every night for several weeks in a row. Thank goodness it would only happen when I was by myself in my bedroom.

This was the extent of my experiences while I lived there. I would hear the occasional bump or bang but was able to debunk each sound as one of my roommates. The noises I heard in the basement were often Sean moving around. He worked unusual hours, plus he was going to college. Chris would also be up at all hours of the night doing schoolwork. We also had a family of cats living in the townhome for a few months. This would explain most of the noises in the living room and kitchen areas. There were five kittens plus two adult cats, a male and a female. The male cat would constantly chase the female all over the townhome while the kittens were constantly playing in the living room. They would run all over the furniture and in the entertainment center.

Somewhere around the fall of 2002, Chris got promoted at work and had to relocate to Indiana. This left Sean and me at the townhome. The townhome felt empty without Chris there. He has such a positive, outgoing energy about him. Sean kept to himself the whole time I lived there. I kept busy working and playing softball and soccer. I would also go to the ice rink quite often. I began to look for my own place. I was tired of living with people. The downside of living with these guys was that they both smoked heavily. They always smoked in the townhome.

After a couple of months of searching, I narrowed my choices down to two complexes. I was looking at the *Pickerington Ridge Apartment Complex* and another complex on the east side of Columbus. I had taken tours of each and was having a tough time making up my mind. I went back to the townhome and went over my budget. Pickerington Ridge was slightly more expensive, but it was in a well-to-do suburb of Columbus. It is located right beside the Pickerington Police Department. It was also a brand-new complex which meant I would be the first person to live in the apartment. After some additional thought and reviewing my finances again, I decided that I would move into Pickerington Ridge when the lease ran out at the townhome. Sean came up from the basement one day and started to talk with me about the lease. I told him that I would be moving out once the lease was up.

In the spring of 2003, I moved into 180 Great Trail Street in the *Pickerington Ridge Apartment Complex* in Pickerington. This is located on the east side of Columbus. They had finished building the apartment building I moved into a couple of months before and had just laid the blacktop for the streets three weeks before I moved in. I was about five minutes from James and Maribeth. I was ecstatic. This would be the first place I ever lived in by myself. They have a pool, 24-hour fitness room, a practice putting green, and an onsite carwash for residents. My apartment was a top floor end unit. I specifically asked for this unit because I worked daily swing shift at Lowe's on Brice Road in Reynoldsburg. My mom and dad came from Pennsylvania to help me pack and move into the apartment. My friend and coworker, Ryan also helped. We had to wash all my clothes three times and let them air dry on my deck to get rid of the cigarette smell. Mom and dad spent the weekend there and helped me finish settling into my new place.

During the first few months, I worked a lot and spent most of my time by myself at my new place. I would occasionally have friends over for dinner. This would include Ryan and his girlfriend at the time, and James and Maribeth. It was a bit of an adjustment to living by myself, but it was worth the small sacrifices I was making to live there. I had finally gained my independence. I had an air of real confidence about me. I had finally established myself. I would go out occasionally for a few drinks with some of my coworkers to help pass the time. The apartment had a great feel to it.

After a few more months, I started to look around for someone to date. I looked for a few months with no success. The women I would ask out were not interested or were already in a relationship. Then one day when I was on my lunch break from work, someone really caught my eye. I would frequent the local restaurants that were close to Lowe's on Brice Road where I worked. There was a particular woman that I became very interested in that worked at Chipotle. She was nice and beautiful. She started giving me free meals on a regular basis.

One day I decided that I would give her my number. I told her I wanted to take her out for dinner for giving me all the free meals. A few weeks went by, and she called me. We agreed to meet at my apartment, and I would drive us to Uno, a restaurant in Pickerington. Dinner ended up lasting about three hours. Then, she realized what time it was and said she had to leave.

We ended up having dinner again and started spending time together. Then one night, she came to my place from work and told me she was going to spend the night. It ended up being a very wild night. This was the start of things to come. She came over more frequently and after several more times, we had a talk and decided that we were in a relationship. I began buying candles and burning them every night when she would come over. My apartment felt like a home now. There was nothing but positive energy in my apartment for several months. We had some ups and downs like every couple, but we remained together for about a year or so. Sometimes I would go to her house downtown. She had roommates that were very jealous of us. There was always a tense, negative energy in the house whenever I was there, let alone spending the night.

One night that I stayed over stands out to me in particular. I was very restless and had tons of anxiety. I could sense that something was wrong and that something was about to happen. I would go to the one window and look at the sky. I felt drawn to that window but would also surveil the neighborhood from the other windows in her room. The one time I looked, there was a bright area in the sky; it was white and lit up a decent section of the surrounding sky. It remained that way for a few hours. It was a steady source of light. When I looked at it, I was almost overcome by a sense of fear. This was during the middle of the night. I felt awful the next day due to lack of sleep. She slept straight through until her alarm went off.

A few months later, we were discussing marriage. I told her that I was raised the old-fashioned way. I would have to ask her parents' permission to marry her. She informed me that her whole family still lived in Argentina. We made the necessary travel arrangements and left for a visit there a few weeks later. While I was there, I asked her parents for their permission to marry her, in Spanish, since they did not speak English. There was a brief discussion between her father and one brother. Her brother went into the house and came out with a cat skin. He presented it to me as a gift. I really did not want to take it, but she told me it would be an insult to her family if I did not accept it. I brought it back to my apartment once we returned from Argentina. Not long after this our relationship was over.

My apartment felt like a vast empty space. Thank goodness for some of my friends. They began to spend more time with me and that helped to lighten my mood and the energy in my apartment. I began to hit the bars and social scene. One of my friends had me drive to a hookah store in a shady part of downtown Columbus in the middle of the night. We started to smoke that and that was the only night she smoked it with me. I would smoke it several times by myself after that.

I became involved with a girl from work. At first everything was all right, but then things started to turn. She became super possessive even though we were not in a relationship. I was always in a state of anxiety when she came to my apartment. This only lasted a couple of months, and I ended this arrangement which helped lift the negativity in my life. I took a bit of a break from the social scene to allow some time for all the negative feelings I was experiencing to dissipate.

A couple of months later, I went to a party on the west side of town with one of my best friends, Jimmy. I ended up talking to a girl at the party and we ended up leaving together. We made the trip to my apartment. Jimmy was waiting for me since he left his keys in my car and had left the party earlier with someone else. She spent the night and then left the next day to return to her house. My life had started to go downhill fast. She was good company, but I decided to end it with her especially after she told she was married to guy in the Army, who was currently serving in Iraq. This was one of many bad decisions I had made in those few months.

I began to isolate myself after this. Lots of terrible things began to happen to me after I called things off with her. My first thought was that karma was paying me a visit. Then I remembered she told me she was a Wiccan. All these things played into the events of the next couple of years. I had become anxious all the time and was showing signs of paranoia.

The first noticeable episode happened when I was dog sitting for James and Maribeth. I would walk their Dachshund named Jackson. I went over to their house one day after work to walk him. They told me I could help myself to food in the house while they were away on vacation. I was planning on cooking myself dinner after I took Jackson for a walk.

When I came back with him after his walk, a wave of sheer terror overtook me. I only stayed in the house for about a minute more. I scooped up Jackson, grabbed his leash and left the house. I took him over to my apartment to spend the night. I have never felt such intense fear in my life. It was like something was there and did not want me there at all.

After James and Maribeth came back from vacation, I told Maribeth about this experience. She could not explain it. She said she had never had anything like that happen to her. It was the first time I ever felt that way in their house. It was always a warm and welcoming feeling every other time I went there.

Then, activity started happening in my apartment. There would be unexplained noises coming from the kitchen when I was in bed. There would be cold spots when I would walk through the living room into the kitchen or bedroom. I thought this was very unusual since it was the beginning of summer. I would always feel like someone was watching me wherever I went in my apartment. I had started to hear voices in my living room while I was there by myself. I tried to explain that as my neighbors talking, but the voices were coming from just a few feet away from me.

The most terrifying event happened one night not long after I went to bed. I was very restless and had been up and down all-night wandering aimlessly around my apartment along with using the restroom frequently. I laid back down in bed on my stomach which was unusual to start with. I laid there for several minutes trying to fall to sleep when suddenly, I was lifted off the bed and thrown against the wall with tremendous force. I ricocheted off the wall back onto the far side of the bed and almost fell onto the floor. I was in dire straits. I had no explanation for any of these events and did not tell anyone because I was afraid, they would think I had lost my mind.

Things continued to get worse for me. I stopped taking care of myself. Somedays I would go work wearing the same clothes I had on the day before. I had not showered and had almost stopped eating. I lost close to 25 lbs. in under a month. I stopped answering my phone. I was ready to give up. The more depressed I became, the more the activity increased. I saw no relief in sight from the things that were happening to me. I would occasionally spend time with my friends Jimmy and Joe and their girlfriends. They were genuinely concerned about me.

One day my parents and brother showed up at my apartment unannounced. After a couple of days, they took me to a doctor. He put me on an experimental antidepressant, Effexor. My parents and brother packed me and my things up and moved me back to PA in the middle of the night.

Back to The Beginning

When I arrived at my parents' house, I was still adjusting to the new medication. From barely sleeping at all towards the end of my time in Ohio, I slept for the first four or five days almost straight through. I would get up to take my medication and get something small to eat and then go back to bed. Cinder would climb into bed with me while I slept. (Cinder stayed at my parents' house while I lived in Ohio because I had roommates for the first several years I lived there and was unable to take him with me while I lived in Ohio). He was extremely happy to see me and would always stay with me no matter where I went in the house.

After my body was adjusted to the new medication, I began to try to do stuff around the house. I started by doing laundry and slowly worked my way up to doing other things. I had many doctor's appointments, both with the family doctor, and eventually, with a psychologist. The family doctor was trying to help with my antidepressant medication and adjusted the level once because my depression was getting worse. I was not able to work during this time because the doctor was afraid that I would have a reaction to the medication. I ended up going on food stamps because I had no money whatsoever.

During this time, I began to have experiences in my bedroom. I felt like I was being hit, bitten, and scratched whenever I tried to go to sleep. I would feel like people or things were climbing into bed with me and sometimes see red eyes in shadow figures in my room or in my bed. The door to the laundry room, (formerly my older brother's room), began to open again. I would catch myself talking in my sleep. I was talking so much and rambling that I would wake myself up. Not much longer after this, the doctor added Ambien to my meds because I was not sleeping.

Most nights when the activity got too bad, I would get in my car and drive around all night. Sometimes when I was driving, it would feel like something would force its' way into my body. I would black out and come to after a period of time. I would still be driving my car but would not know where I was or how I got there. I would be in a completely different area than I had started in when I began to lose consciousness. I would have no memory of driving during this time. I would just come to and had to figure out where I was, sometimes almost swerving off the road.

After this started happening, I would try to fight through the sleeplessness and events. I was extremely fortunate that I was not involved in an accident or hurt anyone. I would consume crazy amounts of energy drinks and all kinds of caffeine to avoid falling asleep. I started cooking in the middle of the night and wandering around the house other nights. I would not remember any of this the following day. My depression continued to get worse, and the doctor added Zoloft and eventually a third antidepressant. The lower I got, the worse and more frequent the activity became.

I began to hear voices and would sometimes interact with them. I mostly would hear the voices when I would go down in the basement, specifically on the stairs. It would be voices of people that I knew. I would have full blown conversations with the voices. I would stay at home and these conversations while my mom and dad went out for dinner.

I began to see people in the house that were not there. I would see them, in some cases my friends, lying on my bed. Other times, I would see people looking at me from around the door frame that led to the living room. It would always be two women. One looked like a friend from college. The other one I did not recognize. They would look at me and then walk towards my parents' bedroom. I would get out of bed and follow them. They would stand beside my parents' bed and poke at my mom. I could see her move in her sleep. Every day after this would happen, she told me that she felt like someone was standing over her while she was asleep. I did not know what to say to this. This happened several times over the course of the next few months.

My dad had me start to do work around the house for him since he was working extra hours. He had to help cover some of my bills since I still was not allowed to work. This caused a great deal of tension in the house. This also further fueled my depression which, in turn, seemed to feed the activity in the house. I began to paint rooms in the house and the porch railings and a cellar door.

One day while I was painting the front porch railings, there was an episode that happened to me. I was painting the railing on the right side (if you were looking at the front of the house from the outside), and the paint started spritzing on me. I took my glasses off because I did not want to get paint on them and laid them on the porch and continued to paint. I stood up and stretched since I was getting stiff and sore from bending over to paint. I stood still for a few seconds and then I felt a heavy hand on my right shoulder that pulled me backwards violently and I stepped on my glasses crushing them. This, of course, led to another doctor's appointment, another unexpected expense, and more tension at the house.

A month or so later, the family doctor took me off Ambien. I guess my mom had called him and told him about the things I was doing in the middle of the night. He was not sure what to prescribe for sleeping that would not have the same side effects, so I just started taking extra strength Tylenol. This did extraordinarily little to help me sleep. The activity in the house continued and increased after this. I started having trouble sleeping again and would toss and turn most nights. I would still go for drives but not as often because I had barely any money left. I started getting dressed and going for walks in the middle of the night. I would be gone for hours at a time without my parents knowing I was gone. I would travel the local back roads, covering several miles a night. I would always manage to get back to their house right before or at sunrise.

During my walks, I would often see visions of my friends watching me while others would grab and hold onto my legs which would hinder me from walking. I would fight and struggle to continue down the road. I would then get back in bed and lay there wide awake until my alarm would go off to take my medication. I was walking so much, that I developed blisters on both feet right on my Achilles tendons. Other times during the daytime when I would go for walks, a spirit of a woman would appear beside me and hold my hand. It helped to comfort me because I had become very lonely and was not having a lot of interaction with people in person.

I would call my friends in Ohio every day or message them several times a day. They would also check on me if they did not hear from me. This helped me keep my sanity together. I wanted to go back to Ohio so badly and spend time with them. Talking with them helped to keep me calm and helped me laugh. If I talked with them long enough, my depression would subside, if only for a little bit. This would cause the activity in the house to decrease for a day or two.

Somewhere around the spring of 2009, I would lie awake at night and would feel like someone was watching me. I would get out of bed and look around the house. No one was around and mom and dad were in bed. I could not shake that feeling. Then one night, I felt drawn to my window. I looked outside and did not see anyone or anything in the backyard. I continued to look around and looked at the warehouse that was just on the other side of the railroad tracks that ran along the property line of mom and dad's house. This building was the property of Zeigler Brothers, Inc. They produced various kinds of pet food.

There was a tower at the one end of the building from where the plant once stood. It had burned to the ground several years before this. I looked up at the tower and saw a man standing on the platform at the very top of the tower. He was looking down at me. I could not believe my eyes. I went outside in the middle of a rainstorm and looked at the tower again. He was still there staring at me. I walked all the way up the backyard and tried to stare him down. It was not long before my dad and my neighbor came and started talking with me. They wanted to know what I was doing standing in the middle of the yard during the rainstorm. I told them there was a man on the tower staring at me. They both looked up there and told me no one was there.

My dad urged to come back inside the house. I had been outside for an extended period of time and had become chilled. He made me a cup of hot tea and told me to go to bed. I went to bed but still could not sleep. I would later tell the prison psychologist this story. I honestly cannot say if she believed me or not.

The tower of Zeigler Brothers Feed Mill in Gardners, PA where I saw the man on the top platform staring at me.

In July 2009, everything came to a violent head. The combination of being overmedicated, my depression, the activity in the house all led to an event. One Sunday after having lunch with my parents and other family members, I came back to the house. I was fighting with rage most of the morning. I had no idea where it was coming from. I remember putting a load of laundry in the washing machine and my parents coming into the laundry room. A tidal wave of violent energy and sheer rage completely consumed me. Once this happened, I have absolutely no memory from that exact time until about several hours later.

The following information was only made known to me because of reading the police reports later. Apparently, I went into a major fit of rage and began yelling at them as loud as I could. I then forced my way out of the laundry room. My dad gave chase while my mom called 911. I reached into the gun cabinet and grabbed a rifle. It was not loaded. A struggle ensued between me and my dad for possession of the rifle. He wrestled it away from me. I then grabbed my keys and went to my car. I drove it around the house where several police cruisers were waiting. I took off at top speed like a bat out of hell and led them on a high-speed chase for a few miles onto a back road where they knocked me off the road. I was arrested and taken to jail. I would spend the next four and a half months in the Adams County Prison.

When I arrived there, I was made to strip naked and put in a heavy weighted jacket and placed in a holding/detox cell. I spent several days there, leaving the cell only to use the bathroom. From this cell, I was then put in a cell by myself. I was in the hole, the most restrictive part of the prison. I spent my time there in solitary confinement on 22–23-hour lockdown. There was no TV or anything for me to do until I asked for a Bible. My only interaction with people was with the correctional officers and the prison psychiatrist. I was interviewed by a local psychologist to determine if I was mentally fit to stand trial. I was put on more medications, an antidepressant and Risperdal to help me sleep.

I became depressed from lack of interaction with people. I started having paranormal activity happen in my cell not long after being put there. The activity started with cold spots in my cell during the middle of the day. This was followed by hearing voices and then I would feel a cat lay on my mattress beside me and I could hear it purr. Some days I would wake up suddenly and feel like I was not alone in my cell. I would sit up in bed and look around. I began to see one of my friends from Ohio sleeping beside me. It was like she could feel me move and would look at me and then disappear. We had worked together at my last job in Ohio and had become good friends. We exchanged numbers and email addresses. We had started texting every day while I lived in Columbus.

Other days I would see and sometimes feel another friend touch me while I was in my cell. Then, I would hear my friends' voices on certain days when I was really depressed. Sometimes they would say good things, other times I would hear them say things like I was not part of the Sand Gnats (a recreational softball team we played on). This would send me into a tailspin.

I was having a challenging time distinguishing what was real and what was the medication or my mind playing tricks on me. I was being tormented every minute of every day while I was incarcerated. This resulted in me banging my head off the concrete block wall until I was yelled at each day by the correctional officer on duty. After I was yelled at, I would then sink into my thin mattress on the lower bunk and would become overtaken by the voices and noises in my cell. I would go into a stupor and would remain like that for hours at a time. I guess you could say I went mad from everything that was happening to me. I was told that I was too dangerous to put in general population. I was also on suicide watch the whole time I was there.

The day came when I went before a judge. I was made to put on a large leather belt. The guards put shackles from my ankles to the belt and from my wrists to the belt. Officials thought I was a flight risk and a danger to others. My public defender waived the preliminary hearing, and I was taken back to the prison and immediately put back in my cell. My public defender advised me to plead guilty to terroristic threats, a misdemeanor, and fleeing and eluding, a felony. I signed the deal and was released in mid-

November, just in time for Thanksgiving. I was then put on house arrest for about four months and had to serve about three years of probation.

As soon as I set foot in my parents' house, the activity started. I started hearing voices in the house when no one was around. I could feel things climbing in and out of my bed besides Cinder. I was seeing people that were not there. I was taken off some of the medications I had been on and was placed on an antidepressant along with Risperdal. The family doctor then decided to run some more tests on me. The results of these tests concluded that I had an overactive thyroid. I was then put on Levothyroxine. The events in the house seemed to slow down some, however I was still in a state of depression. I had no job, could not go anywhere unless I had permission and now, I had no driver's license because of the charges, I had plead guilty to.

One day I was in Walmart in Carlisle with my mom and dad. I was walking near in the main front aisle when I began to get an uneasy feeling. At first, I thought it was from not being around large groups of people. After a few minutes, I began to look around. I felt drawn towards the women's clothing section. I looked and saw an older lady walking through this section. I looked closely at her, and she looked exactly like my grandmother. I turned away for a split second not believing my eyes and looked back. She had vanished. My grandmother passed away several years ago.

I do not have an explanation for this. Some people will say it was someone that looked like her and just walked into another area. This woman was the exact same build as my grandmother with the same hairstyle and glasses. I saw her face and it looked exactly like her. She had her pocketbook over her right shoulder with a sweater over both her shoulders like my grandmother always did. She had started to walk in my direction shaking her head back and forth when I looked away. I believe it was her watching over me.

After applying to over 100 jobs, I finally got a call from a local greenhouse. It was not my first choice for a job, but I did not have a choice. I had to get a job or face going back to jail. It was extremely demanding work. The upside was that there was a soccer field where all the workers would play during lunch time. I started to play every day. I had previously played soccer for a couple of recreational teams, so my skills started to come back to me.

Working hard and playing soccer helped with my depression. My mood really improved once I got my first paycheck. I finally had money to pay bills. This helped to alleviate some of the tension in my parents' house. The activity began to subside for the time being. This job was just a seasonal position, so I worked for a few months and then it ended in late August, I think. I was smart with my money and barely spent any of it except for bills. I was back on the job hunt.

I went a few months without work again. I had bought a tablet and was drawing and making sudoku puzzles. I did sudoku puzzles while I was in prison. I liked how they challenged my mind and kept me occupied for just a few minutes here and there.

Then out of nowhere, I began to write. My first pieces of writing were poems. I hand wrote them with pencil on my notepad. (I later published these poems in my first book, The Longing in 2020 and included a scanned copy of my handwritten manuscript in my autobiography, The Rise, Fall, and Resurrection of Mitchell Ryan Murtoff 2000-present in 2022.).

My dad had turned our gas fireplace on, and I would go into the living room and lay on the floor and write in front of the fireplace. Cinder would come out of my bedroom and lay beside me while I wrote. He also enjoyed the extra warmth since it was getting colder at night. I would write until the middle of night or early morning hours. I found myself more at peace and that helped to ease the depression and anxiety that had developed. I began to sleep better at night and the activity seemed to decrease during this time. I was becoming more stable.

I was browsing the want ads in the *Gettysburg Times* and *The Merchandiser* when I saw Gardners Market was hiring. It was within walking distance of my parents' house. I stopped by and filled out an application. The manager called me the next day and interviewed me. She talked with the other employees about me working there considering my past. They were OK with me working there. She did not tell the owner about my record.

The job was perfect. I walked back and forth to work on my scheduled days and helped dad out around the house on my days off. I was only getting about 20 hours of work a week to start. Things were going well. I had money coming to pay bills and some left over for other things. I had finally gotten my driver's license back and that helped. I was able to drive myself back and forth to the probation office and I would go to get some groceries occasionally. I was meeting lots of new people and reconnected with some friends I went to high school with. All the interaction with people helped me become more open and social. I had become very withdrawn from the four months I spent in solitary confinement.

The owner of the store also owned a store in Carlisle. He was having trouble getting anyone to work there for an extended period. I had asked about getting more hours but there were no hours available at Gardners Market. He asked me if I would be interested in working at both locations. I would get up early and drive to Carlisle and work there until about noon. Then, I would come home and eat lunch and then go to work at the Gardners store.

After a couple of weeks, I joined the local Planet Fitness in Carlisle. Once I was done working at the Carlisle store, I would go straight to the gym and work out, then go home to eat and from there go to work at the Gardners store. This helped to burn off some of the anxiety that I was developing from the new medications and sometimes being overwhelmed with dealing with the public. My body responded very quickly to my training regimen. Within a few weeks, I was built and defined. This started to draw the attention of the local women customers. Many of them openly flirted with me, even though they were married or in a relationship.

Working out and all the attention I was getting really helped with my confidence. I felt better about myself. The activity in the house was almost non-existent. I was sleeping better again. Cinder was sleeping all night now. He was noticing anything in the house.

Around this time, I started to get into woodworking. I began to buy tools and lumber from Lowe's and local sawmills. I started to make designs of furniture for myself and began to build it. I had a few hand tools and corded tools along with some benchtop tools. I had been using my random orbital sander every day for a while.

Suddenly in the middle of the night, my sander turned on all by itself. I would get up and go down to the basement and turn it off. There was no one in the basement. This continued to happen on a regular basis. Some nights, my dad would go down to the basement to turn it off. I really did not know what to think about it. My conclusion was that someone was visiting and trying to help me out. My dad told me that my great uncle Richard had been a woodworker. He had made looms for wool that were being shipped over to Europe. He passed away recently.

My schedule at work had changed. I was now working full time hours at Gardners Market. Around this time, a beautiful woman came into the store. We made eye contact, and the attraction was instant. We would constantly check each other out every time she came in. She was married. We eventually exchanged numbers and became friends on Facebook. We began texting each other every day. After several weeks, these texts became more intimate. Her husband would come into the store and tell me I was all that she talked about. Everything seemed OK.

A few months later, I saw one of her posts on Facebook. Her husband had died. I found out after the fact that he had died unexpectedly. She was devastated. I felt like a piece of garbage. I do not know for sure if that was the cause of it or it had been the last straw. Her post indicated that he had been struggling with depression. Not long after this, I noticed a presence in my room. I became very uneasy and restless. I would wake up and see Cinder staring at the wall where my dresser was. I would look there but not see anything. I could tell I was not alone and whoever, or whatever, was there, was not happy with me at all and wanted to hurt me. I could feel the ice-cold stare generating from the wall. Sometimes, I would feel a cold breeze go right over top of me while I was in bed. It was a very menacing presence. This happened every night for several months. Once she had found someone else, these experiences stopped. I was still very terrified some nights that something bad was going to happen to me.

Then, tragedy struck. One afternoon before I went to work at the store, I saw Cinder's dish was empty. I filled his food dish and gave him fresh water. He had been extra good, so I decided to give him some treats. I always ordered his treats and vitamins through 1-800-PetMeds. They would always send bags of catnip with his treats. I never gave him any. There were several bags of it beside his vitamins and treats. I had forgotten to get rid of it. I opened the cupboard door under the sink where I kept his treats and vitamins. He came over to me like always and caught a whiff of the cat nip. He then jumped in the cabinet and pulled some of it out onto the floor; somehow, he managed to rip open the bags and ate almost two bags before I could stop him. He had never done this before.

Over the course of the next few days, he became very sluggish and stopped taking care of himself. His fur became matted, and he would just lay around breathing heavily. I was going to take him to the vet, then one day he snapped out of it and was walking around the house and acting like his old self. I went to work thinking he would be OK.

Dad called me at work and said he was laying around again and not doing too good. This was not long after I went to work. A few hours later, he called again and told me that Cinder had passed away. I almost ran home after work not wanting to believe what my dad had told me. I went in the back door, went into my room, and found him lying on the floor of my bedroom. I was terribly upset. I had a brief conversation with Cinder the day before when he was not doing too good. He was lying on the floor of the bathroom. I knelt down and told him, "I know you are not doing too good. If you have to go, I understand." He began to breathe heavily right after I said that and that he started to breathe normally again.

I told Dad I wanted to bury him under the maple tree in the backyard with the other pets we had growing up. There are several cats and dogs buried under or around the tree that had died since I was little. He got a shovel, and I took Cinder up to the tree and dug a grave for him. I buried him and said what I thought would be my final goodbye. I went back to my room and cried for the rest of the night. I had him since he was about 8 weeks old. He was about 14 years old when he died. I was alone with my thoughts at night and had a tough time sleeping for several weeks.

The maple tree where Cinder and other family pets are buried. It is pretty fitting that this is the last of the three original maple trees my dad planted when the house was built. At the time of this picture, my dad was in the process of cutting it down since it was rotting and almost ready to fall.

After moping around the house and at work for a few months, I decided to get another cat. I had been talking with John, my coworker at the store, about Cinder dying and how I wanted to get another cat. He thought that would be a good idea. When we were slow at work, he would read the paper and some evenings come and talk with me to make sure I was doing OK. He would show me ads in the paper for people selling cats or giving them away. I could not decide on any of them. Then, he started showing me ads from the SPCA. I saw a few cats that caught my interest.

I had to wait until payday, but it was worth the wait. I went to the SPCA on my day off and went into the cat room. I was looking for a specific cat that I had in mind and was hoping she was still there. I found her. Speckles is a domestic short-hair tortoise shell cat. She had been put up for adoption by an elderly couple that had to move into a retirement home and they were not allowed to have any pets there.

The lady opened the cage for me. Speckles ran out and stood at the other side of the room for a few minutes before approaching me. I met her halfway and put my hand out for her to smell. She started to rub against me. I told the lady I wanted to take her home with me. I went to the desk to pay the adoption fees and the lady behind the desk told me the previous owners had already paid the adoption fees.

I took her home and opened the carrier in the living room. She jumped right out and walked around like she owned the place. When I went to bed that night, she followed me into my room and looked at me and meowed when I climbed into bed. I told her to come up and, after a little encouragement, she jumped onto my sleigh bed with me. She has slept with me every night since. This would prove important later as I found out she was sensitive to paranormal events in the house.

I continued to work at the store for a few more years and continued to buy tools and materials to start a woodworking business. Then, my epilepsy medication took a huge jump in price. I did not have health insurance while I worked at the store. I started to job hunt again. I talked with the plant manager at O'Malley Wood Products that was just up the road a little farther from the store. They offered health insurance. Once they hired me, I put in my notice at Gardners Market and explained why I was leaving.

I began working at O'Malley's the following week. I was working dayshift. This made an enormous difference for me. I had been working second shift at the store for a few years and did not have any life whatsoever, let alone the fact that I was on probation. About six months later, I stopped taking the antidepressant the doctor in prison had prescribed. I missed a dose one day and felt great. I went a few days without it and still felt great. That is when I decided to stop taking it altogether. I told the family doctor I stopped taking it and he flipped his lid. I told him I was doing better without it and refused to take any more antidepressants he would try to prescribe me.

I had built up an inventory of products to go to festivals with my woodworking business. It consisted of wine racks, wine buckets, cutting boards, plaques, humidors, and other items. I booked my first festival at the *A Taste of Apple Country Wine Festival* in Biglerville, PA. This festival was the first day after my probation ended. I had a couple bottles of wine to celebrate. This helped to keep me busy when I was not at work and helped to wear me out, so I slept soundly every night. The activity had ceased almost altogether. The laundry room would open occasionally and my sander would turn on, but that was about it.

I began to play volleyball at Emmanuel Baptist Church again. I would go there every Monday night. We would play for a couple of hours, then I would drive home. It was somewhere during this time that the whole clown scare thing was happening. I began picking up on things when I would drive at night. It was like a heightened sense of awareness. There was supposedly one of the clowns around the area I lived in. I would feel an overwhelming sense of fear when I stopped at a particular intersection on my way home from volleyball. Occasionally, I would see a shadow lurking behind some trees in the woods.

One night when I was coming home from playing volleyball, I stopped at that intersection like normal. I looked for oncoming traffic and this time I saw the shadow on the edge of the woods looking right at me. Then, it started to move towards me. I stepped on it and raced towards my house like a madman. I opened the garage door with my remote opener before I even pulled in the driveway. I parked my car and almost ran up the driveway into the garage and immediately closed the garage door. I unlocked the door, closed it, and locked it. I went to get ready for bed and called Speckles into my room. I climbed into bed, and she jumped on the bed right away. I got comfortable under the blankets, and she snuggled beside me.

About thirty minutes later, I began to toss and turn. I was becoming uneasy and had an overwhelming sense of fear and dread. Then I was laying on my back when a cold rush of air blew over me towards the hallway. My eyes were still closed at this point. During the next couple of minutes Speckles jumped off the bed. I felt someone holding my ankles down and applying pressure so I could not move. I opened my eyes and saw a clown with fang-like teeth staring at me. I closed my eyes and began to struggle, kicking at it, and finally broke free from the death grip it had on my ankles. It finally left go and I felt that the evil presence had left the room. This was the second most intense experience I have ever had right after the experience in Ohio.

Things were quiet for the next couple of nights. Then, I found out Speckles was in tune with things around me. A few nights later, I began to get that restless feeling again. I turned onto my shoulder and looked towards the wall where my dresser and hamper were. Speckles was staring at the wall and would not budge. I looked and could not see anything; however, the uneasy feeling intensified when I looked at the spot where Speckles was looking. This happened frequently over the next couple of months. It was like someone, or something was watching me or almost studying me. I began to think the clown was trying to draw out the fear I had experienced and feed off that to become more powerful. This felt a little different though. I did not have the tidal wave of fear engulf me. Whatever or whoever it was seemed content to just let me know it was there.

Speckles sleeping and watching over me in my bed where most of the activity is centered in my room.

Things began to intensify soon after that. I would feel someone getting into bed with me. I could feel the mattress sinking with the weight of a person pressing down on it. I would look and there was no one there, so I would go back to sleep. Some nights Speckles would jump down from the bed and run out of the room. This person or being would lay there beside me every night for some time. I ignored it figuring it would eventually go away. Then, some interesting events started to happen.

One night not long after I fell asleep, I felt someone lean on my bed and press down on the mattress with both their hands. It leaned forward and kissed me on my left eyebrow. Another night, I felt this being climb into bed with me and I pulled the blankets partially over my face. The blankets were then pulled back from my face and then there were a couple of deep breaths on my face. I looked and saw the blankets being pulled away from my face. Whoever or whatever this was seemed very interested in me. It would climb into bed, and lay beside me, and look at me all night. Speckles would not sleep in my bed during this time.

I remained at O'Malley Wood Products for about three years. While I worked there, there was very extraordinarily little activity in the house. The person or being would occasionally get in bed with me and the door to the laundry room would open occasionally, but that was about it. I then moved onto the Home Depot in Carlisle, PA. I heard the store had some paranormal activity in it but would not experience any until a couple of years later. I started to hear my name being called and there would be no one around me. I thought I was extra tired from working so many hours and I dismissed it.

Then something happened that I could not explain. I was assigned to work on the inventory prep team one year. This meant working the overnight shift. I was walking in aisle 16 of the hardware department heading toward the front of the store when suddenly, I heard someone running towards me from the back of the aisle. As I spun around quickly, the noise stopped right in front of me. I was expecting to see someone trying to play a prank on me and there was no one around.

I would later tell a few other coworkers about this incident, and they told me this happened to several people. Some had even seen a little girl in a white dress in the store after the store was closed or sometimes in the middle of the day. She would appear by herself. When an associate tried to follow her, she would disappear. I was also told at least two people had died on the property before the store had been constructed. Other people reported objects moving on their own or merchandise being thrown off the shelves.

Not long after starting at Home Depot, I became friends with Sky. She helped to train me in the departments I worked in. She eventually moved from Perry County into an apartment in Carlisle with her boyfriend, his mom, and Adam, another coworker of ours. She invited me over several times and all of us would watch TV and drink; other times we would sit around and talk. Sky told me I could come over as often as I wanted to, which I did. It gave me a chance to be around people on a regular basis. Eventually, her boyfriend's mom would move out. This left them with a spare bedroom. I started to spend the night occasionally. This normally happened after a night of heavy drinking. She told me to spend the night rather than risk driving home and getting hurt or hurting someone else.

On one such occasion, I spent the night and was sleeping in the spare bedroom. I slept the whole night until my alarm went off to take my medication. I got up and took my meds and went back to bed. I was laying there and began to get an uneasy feeling. I thought it was just from drinking too much the night before, but then I heard a deep, guttural growl coming from the corner of the bedroom. I looked and did not see anything. There were no pets in the apartment and the downstairs neighbor did not have any at that time either. This remains unexplained, but I am going to say there was the possibility of a demon being near me. I am guessing something had followed me from home or work. It made it a point to let me know it was there. Out of all the nights I spent there (including up to this day), this was the only paranormal experience I had at her apartment.

After this event, activity began to ramp up in my mom and dad's house. Every night there would be movement in my bed. It seemed like it came from something the size of a person or something large. Speckles would stare at the wall and some nights would jump off my bed and run out of my room. I would not see her until the following morning. She began to sleep on the heating pad on the sofa. I knew it had to be something dark in nature if she ran out of the room. I tried not to pay attention to the presence, hoping it would become bored and leave. It was trying to provoke a fear response from me so that it could feed on that negative energy. Eventually, it stopped coming around for some time.

I would talk with Sky about my paranormal experiences. She listened intently and would offer some advice. It helped for me to talk about it with someone that listened to me and did not judge me for these things happening to me and expressing them openly. We discussed investigation techniques and would watch paranormal shows such as Ghost Adventures. This also helped me realize I was not crazy or alone with these matters.

I began to try to communicate and experiment in my house. I had sometimes found myself saying, "I wonder." This would instantly amplify the activity in my room. I could sense multiple beings in my room from cats to other spirits. This would almost put me in a trancelike state. Some nights it would feel like I was leaving the room while laying still. I could almost see my body lying on my bed. I told Sky about this happening, and she told me it sounded like I could astral project. She warned me about this because I was opening my body up to the possibility of possession by the dark energy in my house or something that could be even darker. I heeded her warning and have not attempted that for a very long time.

My woodworking business began to receive lots of orders from my Etsy store. I was spending more time in the basement working. I would be working and listening to music with my headphones on when I started to see things out of the corner of my eye. I started to see what looked like a black cat around Speckles' litter box. I would look again, and it was gone. At first, I thought a stray cat might have come into the basement through an open window. I would leave one of the windows open over-night when I would do my finishing work because the fumes from the polyurethane and lacquer were exceptionally strong. This helped to ventilate the house.

I was taking care of about a dozen feral cats for some time. Other nights, I would see the cat walking around the basement. Then I would start to feel a cat jump onto my bed. I thought it was Speckles, but she was not in my room. One night when I was in the shop working, I saw the black cat and it looked right at me. It looked just like Cinder. I thought I was losing my mind. This was only the first time I would see a departed pet.

Cinder started to appear on a regular basis, and I would feel him jump into bed every night like he used to. I would feel him settle in near my head and he would purr. Then I would feel Speckles jump on my bed. She would lay down a little further towards the foot of the bed. I would tell a few people at work about this and some of my other experiences. One person told me she could get me some sage so I could cleanse my house. I saw this being done on several paranormal TV shows but do not know how to properly cleanse the house.

Some nights when I would lay in bed, I could feel myself talking, but my lips were not moving. I could hear my voice. I started to say the name of all the feral cats that I had taken care of within the past year or so. One by one, I would feel another cat snuggle down on my bed and purr. I was not sure what was happening. This happened several times when I would feel a presence in my room. I was told that cats could be my spirit guide. The spirit cats had not interacted with me up to this point. I could tell they were there to comfort me.

On either Memorial Day weekend or Labor Day weekend, I had the house to myself. I had gone grocery shopping at Giant and was cooking dinner one night. I was grilling a tuna steak and making rice with Saki. I was getting in the refrigerator for some salad and put it on the table. The kitchen was getting warm from the oven being on. I had stepped back from the stove and was getting a drink when the area around me became extremely hot.

The interesting thing about this was that the wave of hot energy was emanating from behind me, from the wall opposite from the stove. It went from right to left. As it passed by me, I felt three claws scratch the whole width of my back. It then became cold immediately after this. My back was burning. I went to the bathroom and took my shirt off. I could see faint scratch marks. Three scratch marks are always the sign of a demon in the area. This was the only time I was ever scratched (so far).

The activity, from the feeling of being watched to someone or something crawling into bed with me, continued and was still focused mostly on my bedroom. Speckles would still stare at the wall and was on high alert for several weeks. One night I was awakened by a ruckus in my bed. I woke up and saw Speckles being rolled around and struggling on my bed. I quickly reached over, put my arm around her and held her close to me. There was something in my room attacking her. I could not see anything at first. I then saw a shadow move away from my bed as I was nearly sitting upright in bed now. I focused all my energy and anger at this thing and though my mouth was not moving, I hear my voice saying, "You will leave now, or I will banish you back to where you came from." I was in a stare down with the shadow. After several minutes, it dissipated. This was the last time I would ever see it.

The wall with my dresser and hamper where both Cinder and
Speckles would stare at like there was something there.

Over the course of the next several months, the activity almost completely stopped at my parents' house. The only things happening were the cat, which I believe to be Cinder, being on my bed and the laundry room door opening. I was getting better quality sleep. Speckles was more at ease now as well. She would jump onto my bed and go to sleep right away and spend the entire night in bed now.

Then, I started to have experiences outside the house. These events started occurring every morning on my way to work. I would be driving and listening to my Pandora station the whole way from the house to work. Things were normal until I got to Toland, a small village just south of Mt. Holly Springs, PA. I would pass the Green Mountain Inn store heading north on Route 34 towards Carlisle, when suddenly, I would drown in a tidal wave of infinite sadness. It affected me so much I would start to cry uncontrollably from that point all the way to Carlisle.

It would really impact me once I passed the pull off for parking for people to get on the Appalachian Trail. This stretch of road from Toland to Carlisle covers approximately six miles. I do not think I can do it justice with my description for the overwhelming amount of sadness, pain, and suffering that I was feeling. I would park my car at work and wipe the tears from my eyes. It would take several minutes for me to regain my composure. Once I stopped crying, I would go to work and, while I did not cry the rest of the day, I still felt the sadness all day long. It affected me my entire shift. The days when this happened, I would barely talk with anyone. Some of my coworkers would ask me if I was OK. I would say yes but I know they knew better. I would not explain this to anyone at work.

This is the location in Toland, PA where I felt the infinite amount of sadness, grief, and suffering. This is the parking area for getting on the Appalachian Trail.

In the last year, I have begun to see more apparitions in the house. They always come from the laundry room and heads toward the living room. They are transparent. I have seen at least six different people in recent months. Along with these sightings, I also experienced an uneasy feeling on one side of my bed when I lay there. This is not the side that I normally sleep on. If I moved to the other side of the bed or got off the bed, the feeling would go away. Then one night, I caught a glimpse of another shadow figure. This one was different from the other one. It had a human head that was flesh colored. I began to see it on a regular basis. There was tension and feelings of anxiety all around me. I was not sleeping well.

This went on for a few weeks until one night I prayed that it would go away, and almost immediately, the energy shifted in the house. It was more positive and relaxed. My sleep pattern returned to normal. One night, I drove to the local sawmill to get some lumber. It was about 7:00 P.M. or later. It was completely dark out. I picked up my lumber and was heading home on the back road when I saw something in one of the yards of the houses on the right-hand side of the road. I saw the same shadow figure from before looking right at me as I was driving. It then turned and started to walk towards that house. As it walked away from me, it turned into a black mist and disappeared. I have not seen it since.

On one of my days off, I was working on one of my previous books. I had opened my closet door to get some things out of it for pictures that I wanted to take for my book. One of these items was the cat skin from Argentina, a gift from my girlfriend's (at the time) family. I opened the closet door and felt the air get very thick and heavy. I was having a tough time breathing. I reached on the top shelf of the closet and pulled the cat skin down. It felt very heavy, and I felt a strange energy resonating from it. It made me feel uneasy. This was the first that ever happened to me.

I had handled it several times in the past but never felt anything like this. I took it out of the bag it was in and laid it on my nightstand. I began to take pictures of it for my book. I then put it back in the bag and returned it to the top shelf of the closet. The heavy, thick air engulfed my bedroom. It was very exceedingly difficult to breathe. It remained in my room until the next day. I did not sleep that well due to poor breathing all night. The next day, everything returned to normal.

Not long after this, I started to see the spirit of the catskin. It started to appear in my room and walk through it and look at me. Then, it started to appear in my workshop. I would watch walk all around my equipment investigating everything. I believe it is watching over me as well as the other spirit cats in the house.

Another night when I was getting ready to go to bed, I noticed Speckles staring at the wall that my nightstand and bed are on. She was locked onto something that was in the corner. I walked around the bed and doorway but felt nothing unusual; however, when I stood on the far side of my nightstand and between the door, I became nauseas. I stepped out of that spot and I felt better. I have no explanation feeling for this difference from one spot to another.

A recent encounter happened one morning when I was coming from the bathroom to go back to bed; I heard a cat clawing the carpet and I immediately thought it was Speckles. She has often done this and still does it to get attention. I looked down at the floor and saw a dark, almost black cat walking towards the hall closet door. It stopped and looked me dead in the eyes and then walked into the door and turned into a dark mist. Another morning I had a vision of one of the feral cats that I used to take care of, standing on the back porch looking at the house. I got out of bed to take my medication and I started to hear a cat meowing. I did not recognize the meow. I looked for Speckles and she was eating while the meowing continued. I went to the back door and looked around the porch and did not see anything.

There were days when I would be working in the basement on orders for my woodworking business, Innovative Designs Unlimited, when I would hear loud, heavy footsteps in the living room right above where I was working. I would run up the steps and looked all through the house but could find no one. This mostly occurred on Sundays when I was home by myself most of the day.

Another recent noteworthy incident happened one night not long after I went to bed. I had just settled in and closed my eyes when I heard whispering in my bedroom. It was coming from beside my nightstand. This is the same spot where I had the uneasy feeling previously. I could not make out what was being said, but it was a male voice. It continued for about 30 seconds or so. I told one of my coworkers about it the next day. She told me that someone had a message for me and recommended that I buy a digital recorder to capture the voice and find out what it was saying.

The activity continues to this day. It mostly involves a cat being on my bed or the occasional visitor lying on my bed with me. The door to the laundry room has stopped opening on its own altogether. I still hear my name being called at work and sometimes I hear it through my headphones while I am working in the basement. It is always a deep male voice.

I will go to the windows in the basement and look outside to see if someone is there, but there is never anyone there. I will also look at the basement door at the top of the steps to make sure my dad is not calling me or someone else had entered the house. The door will be closed and no one is around.

Other times I will become confused with what I am doing or go into a haze or mental fog. This occasionally affects my work and I must redo orders because whatever I was working on did not meet my standards. I have often thought this was the result of burnout or just feeling completely overwhelmed with orders. I would work 40 hours a week at my job plus work on orders when I would get home. Most nights, I would work until about 9:00 P.M. or later. During this past year, I was also in the process of writing two other books. I managed to get them published in late December. Both books are available in the Library of Congress. The titles are: The Rise, Fall, and Resurrection of Mitchell Ryan Murtoff 2000-present, (my autobiography), and a book of short stories about all the sports I played throughout my life. titled, For the Love of Sports.

I started taking time to rest but I would still experience states of confusion. I would forget where I laid tools down, or sometimes, I would just stare off into space for several minutes. I would snap out of it sometimes because I would drop whatever I was holding. The noise would startle me out of the trance-like state, and I would have to refocus on what I was doing. This was sometimes followed by fits of anger. The littlest thing would send me over the edge when I was trying to work on orders. While I admit that I do get frustrated occasionally while working on orders, I do not get that upset normally.

I began to throw things in a fit of rage. There was no explanation for these outbursts. As soon as it hit me, it would go away once I acted out. It was like something was temporarily in control of me. I would then regain control of myself and try to focus on what I was working on. I would find the objects, sometimes pieces of wood or tools the next time I would go down into the basement.

I have even had experiences while attempting to draft this book. I have written most of this book in bedroom, stretched out on my bed with Speckles lying beside me. One day I decided to write at the kitchen table. I had done some writing there for my autobiography and had no issues. I began to write about the darkness that occupied my room when I got a terrible migraine headache. It felt like there was a giant vise squeezing the whole way around my head. The pressure became particularly intense on my temples. I was only able to write for about another five minutes and had to stop.

I put my laptop away and laid on my bed for about an hour. I was out of Tylenol, so I had to battle through the pain. A couple of hours later, the pain subsided. It was like something did not want me to tell my story and make its presence known. After that, I only wrote this book in my bedroom. It is like the energy or presence had migrated to the kitchen. I believe this to be true.

The energy in my bedroom has shifted to a positive environment lately except for one side of my nightstand. I believe this is another spirit that just wants to watch me. As soon as I cross the threshold from my bedroom into the kitchen, I can sense a change. It feels very unwelcoming. Whatever is there does not follow me into my room. When I come back into my bedroom, it feels completely different than the kitchen. This is a recent development. I am not sure what this means. It could be a different entity or whatever was tormenting me has relocated since it could not provoke a reaction from me anymore.

A couple of months ago, (before this book was published), I was in state of deep depression. I had not felt this way since 2008. I was getting concerned about this because it had lingered for several days. One night, after I climbed into bed, I felt a cat jump onto my bed. I looked and did not see Speckles. A few minutes later, Speckles jumped onto my bed. I was lying there staring at the ceiling. This was another low point for me. I was losing interest in everything. I laid there for a few more minutes when I felt a cat walk towards me on my bed and sit beside my head. I looked and saw nothing. Then, the unexpected happened. I felt the cat touch my left shoulder with it's paw. It touched me several times on that shoulder gently. I believe it was letting me know that I was not alone and would stay with me to comfort me during this dark time. My first guess is Cinder was still checking in on me. This happened where he normally slept with me when he was alive. Not long after this experience, my depression subsided.

Some people theorize that certain spirits will come to keep you company or give comfort in a time of darkness. I believe there is both good and evil energy in the house. The good spirits are mostly cats or other people that I have known throughout my life or relatives that have passed on. The negative energy in the house takes pleasure in tormenting me and draws strength from my anguish and suffering. I believe it is losing its hold on me since I do everything in my power to ignore it. My depression has also improved.

I like to think that is the result of cutting back on my drinking and cutting certain people out of my life that were a negative influence on me. I have been resting better most nights since doing this. While I still feel someone or something climbing into bed with me, I have accepted the fact that it is there, and it means no harm. I

have decided that no intervention is needed as of right now. I will
further document events and make decisions based on that
evidence.

57

Conclusion

I know most people will try to discount my experiences by saying a lot of it was the result of the side effects of all the medication I was taking, or the rest is just my mind playing tricks on me. I fully expect people to attack my credibility and question everything in this book or try to explain it away. I know what happened to me was and is real. I have confided in several people, and they agree with me. They gave me, and continue to give me, guidance and have referred me to see other people with abilities or who are considered gifted to discuss these events. I have purchased a digital recorder to further document my experiences. Until then, I hope you have enjoyed reading my book and will investigate any paranormal activity in your life. It is always better to err on the side of caution while investigating the paranormal. Just remember, you are not alone with these types of phenomena nor are you crazy. When these events occur, try to document them, and find someone to confide in that can help explain your experiences to you. The right person will make the proper recommendations to you or refer you to someone that will be able to help you.